The Four Seasons

by George Capaccio

illustrated by Timothy Bush

HOUGHTON MIFFLIN   BOSTON

Which season is the best of all—
winter, spring, summer, or fall?

Fall is when the pumpkins grin.
Piles of leaves reach to my chin!

In winter I can skate or sled.

Cold wind makes my nose turn red!

In spring the flowers start to bud.
I'm covered head to toe in mud!

In summertime, the days grow hot.

I love to find a nice, cool spot!

I like the summer best of all—
except for winter, spring, and fall!